9 Things Graduates

MUST DO

to **SUCCEED** in **LIFE**

DR. HENRY CLOUD

INTEGRITY®

P U B L I S H E R S

Nashville

Published by Integrity Publishers, a division of Integrity Media, Inc.,
5250 Virginia Way, Suite 110, Brentwood, TN 37027.

HELPING PEOPLE WORLDWIDE EXPERIENCE *the* MANIFEST PRESENCE *of* GOD.

Published in association with Yates & Yates, LLP, Literary Agents,
Orange, California.

Scripture quotations used in this book are from The New International Version, copyright © 1973, 1978, 1984 by International Bible Society. Used by permission of Zondervan Bible Publishers.

Cover & Interior Design: Brand Navigation, LLC | www. Brandnavigation.com

Library of Congress Cataloging-in-Publication Data

Cloud, Henry.
   9 things you simply must do to succeed in life / Henry Cloud.—Graduate ed.
      p. cm.
   Summary: "Nine life principles that will help graduates succeed in their life endeavors"—Provided by publisher.

ISBN 1-59145-298-8 (hardcover)

   1. Success—Religious aspects—Christianity.   2. Interpersonal relations—Religious aspects—Christianity.   3. Conduct of life.   4. Youth—Religious life.
   I. Title: Nine things you simply must do to succeed in life. II. Title.

BV4598.3.C56 2005
158—dc22
                                                        2005002451

Printed in the United States of America
05 06 07 08 09 RRD 9 8 7 6 5 4 3 2 1

This book is dedicated to five "coaches"

who selflessly guided me in practicing the Nine Things.

I thank you for your guidance and commitment to me:

Dad, Toby, Peter, Greg, and Tony

Contents

Acknowledgments

Sealy Yates, my agent and friend, for helping "birth" this project, as opposed to several other projects that I did not want to do!

Byron Williamson, CEO of Integrity Publishers, for your love of message and commitment to getting it out there in usable forms. This book is a result of that. And for your support and commitment to my overall work, I thank you.

Joey Paul, for seeing the slant of these ideas and appreciating them enough to push the project through.

Jeana Ledbetter, for making sure the above three guys get along, and "greasing the wheels" of the process.

The Invisible Force of Gravity

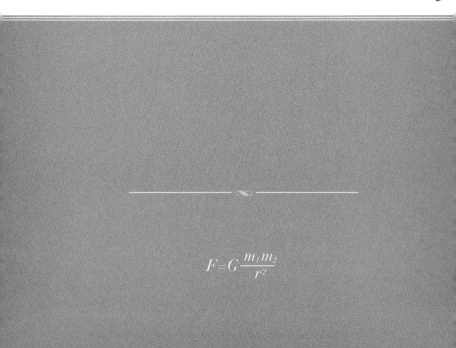

Is gravity hidden? Well, it depends on whether you are flying or falling. Some people are very aware of the law of gravity and use it to their advantage. They design things like airplanes, rocket ships, and satellites. So to those who are flying, gravity is not hidden at all. On the contrary, it is embraced and obeyed.

But there are others who are not so aware. Is the law of gravity hidden to these people? Not at all. Neither are the principles of a successful life hidden from those who fail to practice them.

What I've discovered is that people who found what they were looking for in life seemed to do a certain set of things in common.

They could have learned them somewhere, and they might even have heard of them at times. But to successful people, these things were as real as gravity. Obey them and they will help you do great things. Ignore them and you will fall.

In identifying and observing what successful people had in common, I have discovered nine principles that are like gravity. These Nine Things are there, and we can work with them to achieve great results in success, relationships, love, and other areas of life. Or we can ignore them and suffer the consequences. Now, I would not say that my particular way of communicating these Nine Things is as certain as the proven laws of physics. But what I would say with confidence is this: working with a lot of people who practice these Nine Things has shown them to be utterly dependable. I am convinced that you can count on them to help you avoid hitting the pavement.

OBEY THEM AND THEY WILL HELP YOU DO GREAT THINGS.

An important message of this book is that there is nothing special about the people who practice the Nine Things. Success is not about them or their abilities, or lack thereof. *The truth is that no one is excluded. If you were not born with these patterns, you can learn them.* And if you do not allow failure, past experience, or naiveté to blind you to learning how successful people do it, you can do it too. As Solomon says about wisdom, "Hold onto instruction, do not let it go; guard it well, for it is your life" (Proverbs 4:13).

That is what I believe about the Nine Things: *they are wisdom.* In the upcoming chapters, we will see where they come from, how they work, how to put them into practice, and the pitfalls of not following them.

Are the Nine Things the "ultimate wisdom in life"? I do not think so. First of all, I would never claim to understand the "ultimate" anything. But more than that, I think there are other principles even more foundational than the ones we will look at here. For example, love, truth, and faith are not in the list of Nine. Those are about as ultimate and foundational as you can get. We cannot talk about all of the wisdom in the universe in one book. If you wrote merely a few paragraphs on each of the verses written by Solomon, the wisest man ever, the result would be a volume too stupendous to comprehend in any manageable chunk of time.

I chose the Nine Things for three specific reasons.

First, they are paths or patterns of behavior that really do make a huge difference in the lives of those who practice them. They will pay off.

Second, avoiding these principles can lead to disaster, such as the loss of love, dreams, goals, potential, relationships, and trust—even faith itself.

Third, these principles are often ignored. Yet they are enormously profitable if practiced, detrimentally consequential if ignored, and often overlooked. And they can be learned and mastered, just as you can learn and master the laws of gravity to soar above the clouds at thirty thousand feet.

God provides gifts of wisdom in so many ways. The wisdom we glean through such instruction will help us to find more and more of the life we were created to live. You can put the Nine Things to work for you as do so many others who are no better, no more gifted, or no smarter than you. They simply see gravity, respect it, and let it take them to a higher view.

Dig It Up

Success follows doing what you want to do.
There is no other way to be successful.
— MALCOLM FORBES

"We are here today in an extraordinary building," I said to the audience. "Look at the design, the way it all works. Look at those huge beams that hold it all together and how they majestically stretch all the way across the expanse of the ceiling. The design of this place meets both our appreciation of beauty and our need for protection from the weather.

"Now, I have a question for you. Does anyone know where this arena came from? Where did this building in the real, physical, visible world come from?

"It came from the invisible world of a toddler's soul," I told my audience. "One day, years ago, little Susie, having just learned to walk, was exploring her world more and more. She was in the den one evening right before bedtime, getting in the last few minutes of play. Then, something happened.

"Susie took a few blocks, and instead of her normal pounding them down and throwing them about, she stacked one on top of another. And . . . they stayed! As she stacked the fourth block, something leapt inside her. She laughed with glee. She was so excited to see that a tower of blocks could be built and stay there, one upon the other.

"Her parents encouraged her," I continued. "Later, her teachers encouraged her. When she drew buildings, she felt talent and desire. She learned self-discipline, and she worked hard. And here is the point: this reality, this physical reality of a real structure in the real visible world, came from the invisible reality of a little girl's talent. It came from her soul."

Everything that you can see around you began in the invisible world of someone's soul. It was first a talent, then a dream. It came into being because of talent, discipline, and desire, all invisible ingredients that live in the souls of men and women. A building, a business, a good marriage, and a healthy family all begin in the souls of human beings.

That is the order of the original creation. The visible creation came from the invisible God. He dreamed it, saw it, spoke it, and it was. He has put talents, desires, abilities, dreams, values, and zillions of wonderful things into the souls of humans so that we can bring about beautiful things in life. And they always start from the inside and work their way to the outside world.

Then I told my audience about another building that was just as beautiful as the one we were in that day. We wouldn't be able to find this building anywhere, not in this town or anywhere else. Why? The sad reality is that this auditorium was never built. It is still stuck in the invisible world of another child, one we will call Jenny.

Jenny's initial experience was similar to Susie's. When she was a toddler, she sat on the floor of the den one day and made a similar tower. She felt the same excitement, the same quickening of her spirit inside when she saw the blocks stand one upon the other. She was so excited! Like Susie, Jenny felt alive.

But there was no encouragement from her parents or her teachers. She didn't develop self-discipline, and she didn't move ahead. She allowed her desires to die within her.

Your Heart's Desire

The interesting thing about successful people is that they might have come from healthy families, where the parents were like Susie's, encouraging them to follow what was deep in their hearts and was true to them. They might also come from backgrounds like Jenny's—with dysfunctional families where one learns very little about the principles that help people find success or develop their talents.

ONE THING IS FOR SURE: THE SUCCESSFUL PERSON GOES BEYOND FAMILY BACKGROUND AND LEARNS THE IMPORTANT PRINCIPLE THAT LIFE COMES FROM THE INSIDE.

One thing is for sure: the successful person goes beyond family background and learns the important principle that life comes from the inside.

What lies deep inside is where the real life is. The successful person spends some time listening to it, looking for it, digging it up, and putting it into practice. He finds what lies deep in his heart, below the surface, and invests it in life.

To make a successful life, a successful person:

- Becomes aware of his dreams, desires, talents, and other treasures of his soul
- Listens to them and truly values them

- Takes steps to develop them, beginning in very small ways.
- Seeks coaching and help to make them grow

IT IS OUR INTERNAL LIFE THAT CREATES OUR EXTERNAL ONE.

Principle One can be expanded this way: the reality of the life we see and live on the outside is one that emerges from the inside, from our hearts, minds, and souls. It is our internal life that creates our external one. So, to find our lives we must find what lies below the surface of our skin.

We must look at, listen to, discover, and be mindful of our internal life—of such things as our talents, feelings, desires, and dreams.

Buried Treasure

We don't all seek this internal life because life experiences have made our internal life unavailable to us. Those experiences can come from our family, teachers, friends, church, teachings, jobs, failures, subculture we live in, traumatic incidents, lack of resources or opportunities, and hundreds of other sources. As a result, we find ourselves living lives that are out of touch with our hearts, minds, and souls.

WE FIND OURSELVES LIVING LIVES THAT ARE OUT OF TOUCH WITH OUR HEARTS, MINDS, AND SOULS.

But it is not only in the arena of work or career that this disconnection can happen. It happens in many other areas as well, such as in significant relationships. There are people who merely float along, out of touch with the feelings and drives of their hearts. It is the passion that lies below the surface that makes relationships alive and keeps them growing. Being out of touch with that inner passion can cause a relationship to go stale or even to fail.

There is no shortage of things in life that can cause you to bury your heart and soul.

The truth is, however, that those who succeed in any aspect of life have not allowed those influences to keep their dreams and desires hidden. They have dug them up, faced their fears, taken risks, failed, gotten up again, and found that they could indeed build a beautiful building.

Those who take what they possess, invest it in life, and are diligent and faithful with it over time, grow and build something good. But those who allow fear to keep them from stepping out not only fail to increase what they have, but they actually lose it.

THOSE WHO SUCCEED IN LIFE CANNOT IGNORE THEIR HEARTS, MINDS, AND SOULS.

Those who succeed in life cannot ignore their hearts, minds, and souls.

As Solomon said about minding what is inside the heart, "Above all else, guard your heart, for it is the wellspring of life" (Proverbs 4:23). Success and failure alike arise from what is going on inside, and the wise person is one who pays attention.

**THERE IS VERY LITTLE GROWTH AND REWARD
IN LIFE WITHOUT TAKING RISKS.**

Take Appropriate Risks

There is very little growth and reward in life without taking risks. As the parable says, the one who buried his treasure in the ground did so to avoid risk of loss, failure, and disapproval. In the end, though, he reaped all three of these disasters. Clearly, avoidance of risk is the greatest risk of all.

Taking risks, however, does not mean that when you discover a treasure in your heart you should just roll the dice. As Solomon tells us, "The wisdom of the prudent is to give thought to their ways, but the folly of fools is deception" (Proverbs 14:8).

Growth is when you take the new things that you dig up and discover, and then integrate them with the rest of who you already are—things such as your values, relationships, and loves. A successful person is not afraid of the downside of taking risks. But he does not jump off cliffs and then expect good things to happen. That is what the devil tempted Jesus to do—to give up all reason and rational thinking, jump off the cliff, and hope that God will save him from himself.

To the contrary, risk is calculated, integrated, and then executed with diligence and thoughtfulness. Most people who took a risk and succeeded will tell you that their decision was not flighty or impulsive at all. They made their move only after much preparation and thoughtfulness.

THERE IS A DIFFERENCE BETWEEN BURYING YOUR DREAMS AND SIMPLY SUSPENDING THEM.

Burying Versus Suspending

There is a difference between burying your dreams and simply suspending them. To bury your dreams means to be unaware of them, or to be in some sort of conflict with them. When you bury them, they get stagnant, sick, and begin to

die. That is not healthy.

On the other hand, knowing your soul does not mean that you have to realize or accomplish every dream at once.

Consider a young mother with a law degree and a new baby. She may choose to *suspend her dream*, holding it in the palm of love and sacrifice. She is holding the desire for a law career in her heart along with her heart's other desire: the health and welfare of her child. She puts both desires in perspective with her values and what she knows her child will need from her. That is not burying anything. It is placing her desire for a law career on the altar of sacrificial love, which is the highest form of heart and soul that we know in this life. It is the ability to "lay down one's life" for those he or she loves. She may choose to follow her dream of practicing law at a later time.

No Stagnant Pools

The message is that your heart is an organ designed to have life flowing *through* it. Your mind is like that as well, as is your soul. They are not meant to be stagnant, with things buried in them, stuck there and not moving into the light of the outside world. As you move from the invisible to the visible world, consider these tips:

- Listen to what bugs you. It might be a message.
- Don't let negative feelings just sit there. Do something about them.
- Don't let long-term wishes and dreams go ignored. Find out what they mean.
- Face the fears and obstacles that have caused you to bury your treasures.
- Ask God to help you find your heart, mind, soul, and the treasures he has placed there for you.

DIE WITH FAILURES BEFORE YOU DIE WITH POTENTIAL.

Often, the biggest sign that tells us of things buried in the heart is numbness and a life that is not alive. Grasp your dreams. Reach for them. Take appropriate risks. One of the worst things you can die with is potential. Die with failures before you die with potential. Potential is something to be realized, not guarded and protected.

So dig it up! Invest it! And you will find that it is true— life comes from the inside out.

Pull the Tooth

Buffy: I need to talk to you.

Willow: Good. Cause, I've been letting things fester.

And I don't like it. I want to be fester-free.

— FROM *BUFFY THE VAMPIRE SLAYER*

Principle Two can be described like this: successful people do not hang on to bad stuff for long.

SUCCESSFUL PEOPLE...GET RID OF BAD STUFF.

They get rid of bad stuff. Period. Sometimes quickly and sometimes through a process, but they get rid of it. If the tooth is infected, they pull it. Immediately. They have little tolerance for nagging pains that are unresolved. They get rid of negative energy.

Sometimes this negative energy is generated by the presence of things that are truly negative, such as a significant unresolved problem. At other times the negative energy comes from things that are not innately bad, but simply are not best for the person involved. Thus they become negative influences draining away energy and attention. As problems go, they may seem to be in the minor leagues. But they can spoil your dreams as readily as the big stuff.

Level One: Minor-League Problems

Sometimes things are not bad, but they don't get you anywhere. There is no law against them; they just don't do you any good. As the apostle Paul told the Corinthians, "'Everything is permissible for me'—but not everything is beneficial. 'Everything is permissible for me'—but I will not be mastered by anything" (1 Corinthians 6:12). He was determined not to let even things that were okay have control of him in any way.

There are many such examples that we are not even aware of. Clutter, dead weight, things we keep around that don't help us but take up space or drain resources. Other examples include:

- Relationships you are spending time on that are not going anywhere
- Things you own or are paying for that you are not using
- Time you are spending that is not contributing to your mission in life

This is why we need to do periodic spring-cleaning in our lives, which is basically level one of this principle. You probably

---

WE NEED TO DO PERIODIC SPRING-CLEANING IN OUR LIVES.

---

go through your home, finances, and other areas of life on some regular basis and "clean house." That is normal, and it's a skill we learn as children. Get rid of the things you are not using. They are taking up space and energy, and they are costing you at some level.

Level Two: The Big Leagues

Level two is facing things that truly are negative and either fixing them or figuring out that they can't be fixed and letting them go. What I have learned about the successful person is that he or she does it sooner rather than later.

Sarah was so excited about graduating. The future looked promising and all of her dreams were laid out before her—except one thing. Her relationship with Jason was holding her back and she knew it. He drank too much, partied too much, had little direction in life, and was not always honest with her. She agreed with her friends and family that he was not the person she should spend her future with. Yet she had not made herself end the relationship.

The weekend before graduation, her best friend Ally and she were at a party. Ally asked her if she was excited about the future. Sarah paused, looked away for a moment, and said, "I will be. I just have to do one thing first. I'll be back in a minute." Immediately, Sarah stepped outside and sent Jason a text message. It read, *I would like to stop by your house after this party is over. I will be there about 10.*

When Sarah came back, Ally asked her where she'd been.

"Oh, just had to take care of something first, so I could answer your question honestly. After tonight, I will be very excited about the future. Thanks for asking," she said. "I needed it."

After talking with Jason that night, Sarah did indeed feel like she truly was graduating from a lot more than just school. Sarah "pulled the tooth."

The first of the Nine Things says that the negative things that are buried in a person's heart should not be allowed to remain there. The second of the Nine Things says *pull the tooth*. Once the negative is discovered, it is not allowed to remain. Either the cavity is filled, or the tooth is pulled. Sometimes it is difficult to know when to keep working on something or when to let it go. The successful person is either working on it and not allowing it to remain negative, or she is realizing that there is no hope and moving on.

PULL THE TOOTH.

You don't have to get rid of everything that has negative components to it. (We would have no friends, marriages, jobs, hobbies, or anything else of value if we demanded perfection.) You do have to get rid of the hurtful aspects of those things. You simply must face and eliminate the problem of the ongoing, negative energy. That is the point. Stop the insanity!

Your life is going to be limited or enhanced by how well you develop and exercise these two skills:

1. Your ability to confront and resolve negative things quickly, directly, lovingly, thoroughly, and effectively

2. Your ability to let go and leave behind the things that are not resolvable

This means "pulling the tooth" as soon as you realize something is not going to work. Don't allow yourself to remain stuck in "fix-it" mode longer than is helpful or hopeful.

DON'T ALLOW YOURSELF TO REMAIN STUCK IN "FIX-IT" MODE LONGER THAN IS HELPFUL OR HOPEFUL.

Sarah had good things in her relationship with Jason. But, in the big picture, there were enough bad things that had been in "fix-it" mode for too long. As a result, the whole of the relationship had a negative drain to it. It was not getting fixed, and her life was not going to soar until she let it go.

In marriage, "pull the tooth" means dealing with negative issues that harm your relationship. No marriage will fit the one in your dreams, but when negative feelings and behaviors are addressed and resolved, the delightful things that brought you and your spouse together in the first place are able to flourish. This principle may mean that you don't throw out a relationship because it has certain negative components. Rather, you take steps to get the other person to change some troubling dynamic or behavior. I believe, for example, in the long-term covenant of marriage. Marriages should not be torn asunder. But even in such a commitment where you are not going to end the relationship, there are certain dynamics that you might have to give up on trying to change, at least for a while. Instead, you learn to deal with them appropriately.

Timing Is Everything

Think about this. At what moment do you deal with the "toothaches" in your life? The answer for most of us: when you can do the least about them. When we avoid facing

> **WHEN WE AVOID FACING THINGS DIRECTLY,
> THEY TEND TO GRAB US AT THE TIMES WHEN
> WE CANNOT ADDRESS THEM EFFECTIVELY.**

things directly, they tend to grab us at the times when we cannot address them effectively. For example:

- The boyfriend who lets you down for the hundredth time because he is not committing enough to the relationship tends to get addressed when you are hurt and angry

- Balancing your checkbook before you are overdrawn and hit with insufficient funds fees

- Committing to activities you don't like that create resentment when it's time to attend them

- An unresolved conflict with a friend or loved one that hits you hard when you are away from them, causing crummy feelings that you carry around but do nothing about

- Wishing you'd done an internship now that you are hunting for a job

Here is the sad result of not living like a successful person: you get the negative emotion of all your problems without the benefit of solving them. Avoidance may help you avoid the pain of actually pulling the tooth, but it does not help you avoid the pain. In fact, in the end, avoidance always prolongs pain.

When to Let Go

One of the toughest things to figure out is when to let go of something that is important to you. When do you give up hope?

Melanie had fallen pretty hard for Glen. In fact, she was deeply in love with him, and it was no wonder. He was energetic, smart, funny, loving, creative, and possessed a good sense of values. He gave her a lot of attention when they first met, and she thought, as did her friends and family, that he could be "the one." Everybody was crazy about him.

But slowly she began to experience a pattern. Glen's work and hobbies started to take up more of his attention than she did. She began to doubt herself—her attractiveness, her likeability, and whatever else she could question about herself that might explain his lack of responsiveness.

Finally, Melanie had a serious talk with Glen. He promised to change. When he didn't, Melanie ended the relationship—only to get back together with Glen time and time again.

Melanie kept hoping Glen would change. Wishing, actually. A wish is something you desire and want to come true. You want it with all of your being. But a wish is totally subjective and one-sided and has no basis in reality. Hope, on the other hand, is not subjective. The person doing the hoping has good reason to believe that things will happen. Hope is one of the great virtues in life, right up there along with faith and love. (Check out the thirteenth chapter of 1 Corinthians.) But hope is not a fairy-tale wish; it is

IF THERE IS NO HOPE FOR WHATEVER IT IS YOU ARE CLINGING TO, LET GO OF IT.

bedrock, and you should be able to order your life with it at your side. If there is no hope for whatever it is you are clinging to, let go of it so you can be open to something new and life-giving.

Pulling the tooth—getting rid of the painful problem—actually opens the door for new and better things.

The main difference between persevering with a problem and the "bad tooth" issue is twofold. First, any problem is a "bad tooth" if it is not being addressed. If it is just sitting there, without us doing anything to make it better, then it is only getting worse. Very few things in life remain in neutral. Usually they are getting better or getting worse. So waiting it out or persevering without taking steps to make it better is actually avoidance.

The second difference is that perseverance occurs when there is reason to hope and reason to believe that continuing to try is going to make a difference. This is one of the greatest qualities of high achievers: to persevere in difficulty. But to continue to persevere for no good reason may be little more than denial.

The Cringe Factor

I hope you are getting the picture that the wise way to live is to put an end to negative things that are using up your space, time, energy, and emotions. But there is another way a successful person deals with negative problems and energy drains that is even more effective than fixing them or pulling the tooth: *he does not get into them to begin with.*

RESIST THE IMPULSE TO SAY YES.

Solomon gives us a great proverb about the cringe factor: "A prudent man sees danger and takes refuge, but the simple keep going and suffer for it" (Proverbs 22:3). When your senses tell you that something is wrong, there is a reason you feel that way. Check it out to see if it is paranoia or wrongful suspiciousness on your part first. If not, then listen to your senses. Don't be like the simple or naive who keep going and suffer for it. Because you will suffer. How much depends on how bad the tooth is. Resist the impulse to say yes when you feel that cringe of hesitancy or warning.

Make the Appointment

Successful people would give you one piece of advice about your aching tooth. Make the appointment. Pull the tooth. Deal with whatever is wrong. That may mean fixing it, or it may mean getting rid of it altogether.

The overriding principle is that unresolved issues are a drain that will keep you from reaching your goals. That principle does not negate patience, longsuffering, hope, or working out difficult relationships over time. It includes all of those things, doing whatever you can to fix what is wrong and make it better. Forgive and reconcile. But it also means not to let bad situations sit, stagnate, get infected, and drain away your life. "A cheerful heart is good medicine, but a crushed spirit dries up the bones" (Proverbs 17:22). Move quickly to deal with whatever is crushing your spirit.

Pull the tooth.

Play the Movie

The day shall not be up so soon as I,
to try the fair adventure of tomorrow.

—SHAKESPEARE

Successful people rarely take any action without considering its future implications. But not just that. They do not think about how something will impact the future only when making big, scary decisions—almost everyone does that. Successful people tend to think that way *all the time*, in matters large and small. So here, then, is the third of the Nine Things. We've learned that we must dig up and invest our talents, and move past the negative. Now we see that successful people know how each of life's "scenes" contribute to the film's good end.

Principle Three views every behavior as a link in a larger chain, a step in a direction that has a destination. *If I do* A, *then* B *will happen.* Actually, it is more than that. *If I do* A, *not only will* B *happen, but* C *will do. And* D *and* F *and* G... Successful people see this link in both possible directions, the good *and* the bad. They think this way to attain the good things that they want in life, and they think this way to avoid the bad things that they do not want. In short, they rarely do anything without thinking of its ultimate consequence. They *play the movie*, so to speak.

Playing the movie means never seeing any individual action as a singular thing in and of itself. Any one thing you do is only a scene in a larger movie. To understand that action, you have to play it out all the way to the end of the movie.

ANY ONE THING YOU DO IS ONLY A SCENE IN A LARGER MOVIE.

After viewing the entire film, you can decide whether you really want a particular scene in the movie of your life. If it alters the plot or takes you to different scenes or a different ending than you desire, then you do not want it. Conversely, if it creates later scenes that you would want to live out, then you might indeed want to add that scene.

The Future Will Come

Mary dreamed her entire life of being a lawyer. When I met her, she worked in a loan office. "I hate it," she admitted. "Every day I wish I were doing something different, especially practicing law."

"Why don't you do it?" I asked.

"Well, obviously I would have to go to law school, and that would just take too long," she said.

Usually law school takes about three years, which didn't seem like a long time to me when one was thinking about a lifetime of work. I asked Mary to confirm it would take three years, and then I challenged her.

"Okay, think about this. Three years from now will come, and it will pass. Since that day is going to come three years from now, on that day do you want to have a law degree, enabling you to do something you love? Or do you want to still be hating your life? What do you want your life to look like on that day?"

She began to catch on to the script of the movie. She could see that choosing to avoid school was not just an isolated decision. It was only one scene, but the movie was going to keep playing regardless, and that scene would dictate the way it turned out. The movie is not optional, but where the plot line goes is. She could choose to be in a very different movie, one that she would like. Or she could choose to be in the one she did not like at all. It was up to her.

When we think of a difficult thing to do, like attending graduate school or changing careers, we often just think of the immediate comfort that comes from not doing it. *No, I won't do it* gives a little relief from the big gulp of work that school would be for three years. But that is a big lie we tell ourselves—a lie that hides the future consequences of our choices. Yes, you avoid the work. That feels good at the moment. But in doing that, you have made another choice as well: *to have a life you hate three years from now.*

Two Sides of the Same Coin

Wise people play the movie to prevent negative things from happening as well as to increase positive things in life. And by doing so, they can change behavior that they would not otherwise be likely to change.

In addition to motivation, playing the movie provides successful people with another strategy common to all of them. They use it to live out the difficulties before they actually occur. They "borrow trouble," in a way quite different from worry.

WORRYING IS BORROWING WITH NO PAYOFF.

Worrying is borrowing with no payoff. Worry is often the nonacceptance of situations that you cannot do anything about. But successful people borrow trouble from tomorrow in situations that they *can* do something about. They worry ahead of time—they play the movie—and then they take active steps to make sure they are ready when that scene arrives.

A. J. had promised himself that upon graduation he was going to buy a new car. It would be his reward to himself. He figured out the payments, and with his new job, he could afford it. It was set in his mind. That is, until he borrowed trouble in the right way and played the movie.

"What if I get out there and want to make a job change in two years? What if I don't like it? I will be stuck because of a car payment. I don't want to lose my freedom; I want to be able to make the career options that are good for me without being locked to some car payment. I think I will wait on the new car and get a cheaper, used one until I know I am settled."

A. J. felt much better, but more importantly, he felt free and in control of his future. He was in position to write the script.

Not All Movies Are Bad

For every bad movie that follows a pivotal scene, there is a good one that can follow if that scene is rescripted.

One of the best examples of this procedure is Tiger Woods, who grew up with Jack Nicklaus's major tournament record pasted to the headboard of his bed. It was the first thing he saw every morning and the last thing he saw at night. He was playing the movie of his future, winning major tournaments, becoming the next king of golf. And now we are seeing that movie unwind as reality before our eyes. When tempted to skip practice or to sleep in, he could see that none of those immediate scenes would take him to the end of the movie that was posted on his headboard.

On the Big Screen

Plot a movie, a vision of your starring character, your relationships, your spiritual life, your career, your health, your finances. See it, plan it, and then evaluate each scene you write every day in light of where the movie is supposed to end. If you do that, and make sure that you include the right supporting cast along the way, I will be so happy for you when you get your Oscar for a life well lived. "Well done, good and faithful servant!" (Matthew 25:21).

**THE BEST REWARD IS THE LIFE ITSELF,
THE LIFE YOU HAVE BUILT OVER TIME.**

And the cool thing is that the accolade is not even the best reward. The best reward is the life itself, the life you have built over time. That is the reality that will not only last for eternity, but will also give you abundance and fulfillment along the way.

Choose the right scene at each pivotal moment, and you'll be the star in a great movie. One scene at a time.

Do Something

You miss 100 percent of the shots you never take.

— WAYNE GRETZKY

Principle Four is a biggie. The fourth of the Nine Things successful people do in love and life says to ask yourself this question: *what can I do to make this situation better?*

Successful people have a certain quality. In addition to listening to their heart's desire, getting rid of negative stuff, and thinking of how the present will affect the future, they do something else. They tend to turn to themselves as the first source to correct difficult situations. It does not matter whether they think they are to blame or not. Even if someone else is at fault, they will ask themselves, *how can I make things better?*

Whatever the answer, *they make a move.*

MAKE A MOVE.

Are You Driving Your Life, or Just Along for the Ride?

Proactivity

There are many different ways to look at this principle of *making your move.* For example, you may have heard some people described as *proactive*. That term usually means taking positive, initiating steps in life as opposed to merely reacting to situations. If they want a situation to be better, proactive people see themselves as part of the solution, or at least as a catalyst to get it going.

**PROACTIVE PEOPLE SEE THEMSELVES
AS PART OF THE SOLUTION,
OR AT LEAST AS A CATALYST
TO GET IT GOING.**

Dependency

One way to look at this principle is in terms of *dependency*. People who approach life with an attitude of dependence tend to be less successful. This does not mean that depending on others is a bad thing. The problem comes when the dependency is passive, and we look to others to do what we should be doing ourselves.

Ownership and Responsibility

We aren't talking about the kind of responsibility that you

think of in terms of "doing your duties." We often think of being responsible as equivalent to taking out the trash or doing your taxes on time. When things need fixing, who is at

---

NO SUCCESSFUL PERSON NEEDS TO BE TOLD,

"IT IS YOUR LIFE!"

---

fault is not the big issue. What is an issue is being responsible in terms of *ownership*. To own my life means that it is mine and no other person's. I can assure you, no successful person needs to be told, "It is your life!" They know and live accordingly. I can blame no one for what I do with my life. Even when I am wronged, I can blame them for what they do to me, but *I cannot blame them for what I do with what they do to me.*

The Gift of Freedom

Ownership and responsibility may sound overwhelming. Isn't life supposed to be fun? Sure. You even have brain chemicals that help you feel good. And few things feel better than freedom. So how does one find freedom? That is the good news that follows the "bad news" of ownership and responsibility.

Think of how wonderful it would be to gain freedom in relationships, finances, morality, spirituality, feelings, attitudes, career, addictions, or stress.

FEW THINGS FEEL BETTER THAN FREEDOM.

Well, there is no freedom apart from responsibility and ownership. Think of a house. You are not free to do what you want with it unless you own it. And since we can't really be mere guests in our own lives, ownership and responsibility are the only paths to personal freedom. When we stick to these paths and gain freedom, life becomes a joyous experience.

Your Move in Action

What does making a move look like? Suppose your dating life is not working. You could:

- Ask the people who know you what there is about you that may be contributing to things not working out

- Deal with dependencies that render you unable to say no to the wrong kinds of people
- Get out and get involved in activities that would expose you to new people who like what you like
- Deal with your narrow categories that are ruling out potential dates by looking only for a certain type of person
- Get honest about your physical appearance and take ownership for how that might be limiting your chances
- Do the same thing with your personality or habits

**IF THE ECONOMY IS LOUSY,
DO NOT WAIT FOR IT TO CHANGE.**

Compare the people who actively do the things in these examples with the ones who sit and complain, stuck in their misery and wishing that someone in particular or life in general were treating them differently. I have seen lives transformed when people begin to adopt the strategy of asking themselves, *what can I do to make this better?*

If the economy is lousy, do not wait for it to change. Gain a skill in a different field, look somewhere else, find another niche that is hot, enlarge your network or openness to other jobs, start your own business. Do not just sit around and wait.

Tony Thomopoulos was a shining example of someone who did not just sit around and wait for a career. His was the classic mailroom-to-president story: the president of ABC television, that is.

Tony graduated and went straight from school to the basement of a big corporation. He intentionally chose the mailroom over other entry-level positions, because he knew that delivering mail would put him in contact with every department. He would meet everyone in the company, understand all the jobs, and be better equipped to work his way up. He then set a goal to be involved in a certain division by a certain date. He determined he would take any job in that department. But if he did not make it into that division by his goal date, he would leave the company and seek a career elsewhere.

Tony learned of a two-week fill-in job in his chosen

department that would be from 4:30 to 8:30 a.m. He got it and did his best, including researching what the work entailed, arriving one hour early each morning, and finding ways to be of true service to his boss (instead of just trying to make himself look good). Two weeks later, the division chief was so impressed he hired Tony. Tony says he can see that God was involved in every step, but don't miss that Tony also used the talents and work ability God gave him.

The Created Order

I believe that God created the earth and all that is in it, and then he created us. He created us in his image, and we were designed to do basically the things that he does, just in much smaller measures. God did not put us on the earth to fail to reflect his likeness. He did not plan for us to sit back and allow

---

**GOD DID NOT PUT US ON THE EARTH
TO FAIL TO REFLECT HIS LIKENESS.**

---

life to follow the course of least resistance, becoming miserable, oppressive, unjust, full of mistakes, unloving, poverty-stricken, ugly, lazy, negative, and evil without moving to do something about it. Such passivity is as far from reflecting the image of God as one could imagine.

To the degree that we allow life just to happen and are not active forces to change whatever situation we find ourselves in, we are not living up to our true purpose by reflecting God's nature. And that may be the reason you are stuck and not getting to where you want to be.

YOU CAN REST ON THE SEVENTH DAY, BUT DO NOT SLEEP THE WHOLE WEEK LONG.

So get with the program! Be who God created you to be. You can rest on the seventh day, but do not sleep the whole week long. Get moving and *do something*!

Act Like an Ant

Inch by inch's a cinch . . . yard by yard it's hard.

—ANONYMOUS

So far our successful friends have taught us that life comes from within, and we mustn't hang on to negative stuff. They think of how actions affect the future and ask how they can make things better. But little would I have guessed just who (or what) would show me the fifth of the Nine Things we need to follow to be successful. I'll explain.

There was a point in my life when I faced what seemed to be a very difficult task, and I really did not know how I was going to accomplish it. I felt like I was being asked to leap over the Empire State Building flatfooted.

The task was to write a doctoral dissertation to complete a PhD degree. I was the kind of person, at that time, who just did not think in terms of sequential tasks with outside structure. I had no problem with work and study—I always got my work done—but I was not good at developing a structured program on my own to accomplish the many and varied tasks that a dissertation required. I did not know where to start.

So I did what I had learned to do whenever I don't know what to do: I prayed. I asked God to help me, because I knew I did not have a chance of getting this thing done on my own. At some point I was led to open my Bible. Here is what I found:

Go to the ant, you sluggard;
consider its ways and be wise!
It has no commander,
no overseer or ruler,
yet it stores its provisions in summer
and gathers its food at harvest.

—PROVERBS 6:6–8

I looked at the passage again, wondering how in the world this was going to help me with my dissertation. Ants? Watch them? I always just sprayed them. Then a friend bought me an ant farm. I felt a little silly, as most ant farms are probably purchased for eight-year-old kids, but I set up the container, and after the ants came in the mail, I poured them in.

Of course, you can guess what happened, so I will fast-forward. An entire ant city was being built. It had hills and valleys and a complex network of tunnels, which was amazing. It looked like a team of architects and construction crews had been there for months with miniature bulldozers, trucks, and cranes. But when you looked at any given ant, it carried just one little grain of sand. The activity of any individual ant seemed to have little to do with the big picture of what was forming.

The reality was that many tiny ants had taken many tiny steps—one step at a time, one grain of sand at a time, one day at a time. And voila! A city was built. It hit me and hit me hard. This entire amazing feat was really no more complex than one ant with one pebble. One step at a time, one grain at a time.

Suddenly it became clear how to get a dissertation done: one grain of sand at a time, one brick at a time, one step at a time. If the ant could do it, I could too.

ALL-OR-NOTHING THINKING KEEPS PEOPLE STUCK IN DESTRUCTIVE RUTS.

Not too long after that, a dissertation appeared in my hands. What seemed impossible for me had been done. How? Through Principle Five. Just like Henry Ford said: "Nothing is particularly hard if you divide it into small jobs."

But I Want It All . . .

If the ant picks up a grain, the city will get built. But if the ant looks at the grain and says, "That is not a city! What a waste of time!" there will be no city in the end.

All-or-nothing thinking keeps people stuck in destructive

ruts. It certainly is a part of the reason that people fail to practice the Nine Things and become successful. All success is built

---

THE SHORTCUT IS ALWAYS
THE LONGEST PATH.

---

and sustained just like a building is built, one brick at a time.
But one brick seems too small and insignificant for all-or-
nothing thinkers. Successful people are different. They value
the little increments, the tiny steps.

But I Want It Now . . .

Closely related to *I want it all* is its sister, *I want it now!* In my first
book, *Changes That Heal,* I wrote that the shortcut is always the
longest path. People go on crash diets as a shortcut but always
gain the weight back, and more. Others take the approach of the
ant, losing one or two pounds a week, exercising one day at a
time, keeping to a day-by-day life change, and they keep it off.

People have problems like depression or anxiety and want
a quick fix. So they think a few visits to a counselor will do the
trick. But soon they are right back where they started. Others
see a counselor weekly for a few years, or join a support group

that meets weekly, and in a few years their entire lives are different. Not the quick fix, but the one that works.

Some people want to get rich quick through some scheme, the shortcut. But after twenty schemes, at age thirty they are broke. Others built a solid career one step at a time, either through more school or entry-level jobs that led to bigger ones one at a time. At thirty, they are financially sound.

**WANTING IT NOW KEEPS YOU
FROM HAVING IT AT ALL.**

Some want instant intimacy and love through immediate romance and sex. They believe the butterflies. But the ants know better. Long-term relationships and lasting love are built one day at a time, one act of love and communication at a time, one conflict resolution at a time.

Wanting it now keeps you from having it at all.

What Are Your Ant Farms?

Life is what happens to us while we are making other plans. But too often we get overwhelmed, when the obstacles we see standing between us and our goals loom too enormous to tackle.

From now on, whenever you see an obstacle in front of you—and you will, I promise—remember what you have just accomplished. You graduated! Think of how many thousands of obstacles you encountered from the time you started until you finished your degree. You negotiated each one of them, one at a time, and here you are. Life will be just like that.

Save money a few dollars at a time. If you are in sales, build a portfolio of clients one call at a time. If you are out of shape, exercise for ten minutes a day for one week, then go to fifteen minutes, then on up from there, one step at a time. If you are single and dating, do not expect instant romance or love. Successful relationships and marriages are built one minute at a time. One grain of sand at a time. One conversation, one lunch, one act of sharing, one sacrifice, one meeting, one new person, and so on.

And as time goes on, you, too, will succeed, and others will look at you and say, "I can't imagine how he or she did that! What an accomplishment!" You can just look at the ant and say, "Thanks!"

Hate Well

Certain things, if not seen as lovely or detestable,
are not being correctly seen at all.

— C.S. LEWIS

We've looked at ways successful people focus on their internal drive, tolerate no negative energy, make decisions in the present depending upon how they affect the future, take responsibility and take action, and make progress one step at a time. Now we look at the sixth of the Nine Things: the ability to *hate well*.

Why We Hate

Principle Six's concept of hating well may seem like an oxymoron. We usually think of hate as a problem to be solved. We try to get over hatred because we have all seen the destruction that it causes.

In reality, though, hate is one of the most important aspects of being human. It is one of the most crucial ingredients of a good person's character. *What we hate* says a lot about who we are, what we value, and what we care about. *How we hate* says much about how we will succeed in love and life.

What We Hate Defines Us

We are defined in part by what we love and what we hate. What we love says what we will invest in, go for, move toward, give time and resources to, and orient ourselves toward with the best parts of who we are. You can tell a lot about people by what they love. You think differently, for example, about someone who "loves his

---

**WHAT WE HATE SAYS A LOT
ABOUT WHO WE ARE . . .
HOW WE HATE SAYS MUCH ABOUT
HOW WE WILL SUCCEED.**

---

family" as opposed to someone who "loves to win at all costs." What would you think, for example, about a person who said that he hates the following things: arrogance, lying, innocent people being hurt, harmful schemes, evil practices, telling lies about others, and things that stir up dissension among people?

If a person said that he hated those things, and his life demonstrated the truth of his claims, wouldn't you be inclined to like that person? Even trust him?

Character is in part formed by what we hate, because we move to be different from whatever that is.

Our Hatred Protects the Good

The second way hate benefits us is that it causes us to protect what we value. We hate it when things we love are threatened, so we move to protect them. In that way, hate is a protective emotion, urging us to stand for good things.

The third way that hate is a good thing is the flip side of protection. Hate moves to destroy bad things, which are often the things that threaten the good. The hate of evil protects the good not only by shielding it, but also by moving to get rid of it as an act of love. As the apostle Paul wrote, "Love must be sincere. Hate what is evil; cling to what is good" (Romans 12:9).

HATE IS PART OF THE IMMUNE SYSTEM OF YOUR SOUL.

Hate is part of the immune system of your soul. Your physical immune system is an amazing part of your body's makeup. When a bacteria or virus invades your body, your immune system identifies it as harmful and moves against it immediately. Your immune system has a cell that tells the rest of your cells, "This is a bad bug. Kill it!" The evil cell is immediately surrounded, giving protection to good cells. Crisis prevented.

This is what hate does. In the same way that your immune system hates infection, the hate within your character identifies things in your life as evil. So hate the things that destroy life, and move against them when they appear. Hate deception, lying, destructive behavior, hurting innocent people, and like things that only bring pain (Proverbs 6:16–19).

How We Hate

What we hate is important in defining who we are and what we stand for and against. But another important aspect of hate is *how we hate*. Successful people hate in a certain way. They can be depended on to hate in a way that *solves* problems as opposed to *creating* them.

Successful people move against the problem and show love and respect to the person at the same time.

Hating Unwisely

Unresolved hatred can cause all kinds of wrecks and destruction. Like an autoimmune disease that attacks the body itself, so hate can be turned within and produce addictions, depression, anxiety, illness and disease, paranoia, lack of trust, confusion, inability to reach goals, and a host of other destructive results. It has a life of its own, and it runs counter to the goals of those who carry it around. Turned outward, it can destroy relationships and careers.

For example, if someone has been hurt by controlling people and hates feeling controlled, he may explode irrationally at another person when he feels even the least bit

---

HATE IN A WAY THAT SOLVES PROBLEMS AS OPPOSED TO CREATING THEM.

---

threatened or controlled. So it ruins his relationships.

The answer is to make the subjective hatred objective. Let me explain, subjective hatred blasts other people, causing overre-actions, inability to resolve conflicts, and broken relation-ships. If has a life of its own and works against the best efforts of the person who carries it around.

Transform that hatred into objective hatred, which is the kind of hate that solves problems, protects things you value and stands against the things that you do not want in your life. To do this requires finding the real objects of hate (i.e. loss of control), making them specific and using objective measures to deal with them productively. This takes rage and venting at others out of the equation. It is what successful people do. And they do it not with a hateful attitude, but with one that is respectful of others, yet firm.

Assessing What You Hate

Our hate certainly has deep connections to the heart and spurs all sorts of feelings, but it is more than that. It is a stance *for* the most vital things in your life and a stance *against* the things that would destroy them. Most of these vital things in our lives seem to be universal values. In the following scripture, God describes seven things he hates. It shows how *hating well* displays exemplary character:

> *There are six things the LORD hates,*
> *seven that are detestable to him:*
> *haughty eyes,*
> *a lying tongue,*
> *hands that shed innocent blood,*
> *a heart that devises wicked schemes,*
> *feet that are quick to rush into evil,*
> *a false witness who pours out lies*
> *and a man who stirs up*
> *dissension among brothers.*
>
> —PROVERBS 6:16–19

King David wrote in Psalm 101:3–7 (my paraphrase) about how life would be different if hated well: "Whenever I see destructive behavior, I am going to leave the scene. I won't trust people who are betrayers so I won't be walking around with a lot of hurt. I will stay away from people who twist good things such as love or sex and use them in some impure way. I won't play that game. I don't want to be close to those who are slanderers and put others down. And those arrogant types who think they are so superior and try to put me down can just stay away. I want to be around good people with good hearts and spend my time with them. I want to receive what they have to offer. I won't be around liars and people who are not into truth."

There is no rage in those lines of David's—no screaming or ranting. He is just saying, "My immune system is not going to tolerate this stuff in my life. Period." Nonparticipation is the ultimate hatred! No ranting or raving needed—just a very clear stance.

So what is on your list? What is worth hating? And where has hate gone awry for you? What do you hate that is really not "hateworthy"? Where has subjective hate filled you up so much that it finds expression in ways and at times that are not good for you or for others?

Mix Hate with Love and Respect

A successful person integrates his hate and his love and other values, such as respect for people, kindness, and forgiveness. That is how he can take a hard stand on a tough issue but remain loving and kind in the process. You can take an absolute stand against something without being destructively

TAKE A STAND AGAINST WHAT YOU HATE.

BUT DO IT WISELY.

angry. Take a stand against what you hate. But do it wisely. Do it well. Hating well always means lovingly, kindly, being soft on the person but very strong on the issue. Not strong by being loud or angry. Strong by being immovable on the issue you hate.

Destructive or Constructive?

Whether you are going to hate is not an option. You have been created in the image of God to stand up for life and to stand against things that destroy life. So when hurtful things happen, you are going to have a response. It is hardwired into you. The question is this: will that response be *constructive* or *destructive*?

You can learn the pattern of hating well. In the process, you will preserve most of the good things in your life, eliminate most of the destructive things, and experience much more success in both love and life.

Don't Play Fair

An eye for an eye makes the whole world blind.

— MAHATMA GANDHI

There is one thing you can do that has the potential to ruin every relationship in your life.

Play fair.

THEY KNOW WHERE FAIR GETS THEM, AND THEY WANT BETTER THAN THAT.

Successful people succeed in love and life because they do not just play fair. They know where fair gets them, and they want better than that.

Up to now we've looked at how successful people know that you must listen to your heart's desire, eliminate negative forces, choose the future by acting well in the present, take action and responsibility, take small steps to victory, and hate the right things in the right way. Now let's look at the seventh of the Nine Things you must do.

Tit for Tat

Sally and Jen had just gotten a new apartment together. On the day they moved in, they had a big party planned. Sally had promised to take the rent checks to the manager's office, and Jen was going to do some errands to get the food for the evening. She also promised Sally that she would pick up her outfit at the dry cleaners for the big event.

At midday, Jen walked through the kitchen and found her check still sitting there. She wondered what had happened. So she called Sally on her cell phone. Sally said, "Oh, I took mine but I got busy and didn't have time to swing by for yours. They're waiting for you to bring yours so everything will be cool."

Jen was ticked. They had a deal. She felt let down. *Fine,* she thought. *But don't expect your dress to show up tonight. Fair is fair. If mine does not matter to you, then yours shouldn't matter to me.*

That night things did not go well. Sally had nothing special to wear and was upset. When she expressed her feelings to Jen, Jen just said, "I understand. That's how I felt about the check. Hey, but that's fair. You didn't have time for mine, and I didn't have time for yours. No biggie."

It was a biggie. It was a crack in their relationship. From that point on they didn't trust each other, and it only got worse as the doctrine of "fairness" continued to play out. In a few months, they were looking for new roommates. Perhaps they treated the new ones better than "fair."

The Philosophy of the Masses

The problem is that in operating by the principle of playing fair, all it takes for any relationship to go sour is for one person not to perform, and then the other one will do the same.

There is an interlocking dependency: the other person must be good so I can be good. In this kind of dynamic, we need the other person to be loving in order for us to love them, or to behave maturely in order for us to behave maturely toward them. And no one ever performs perfectly, so that is why all it takes to drag a relationship down is one failure. Under the "play-fair" system, deterioration is inevitable. See if these examples sound familiar:

- One person is a little withdrawn, so the other feels abandoned and gives the silent treatment.
- One person is a little sarcastic, so the other one is sarcastic in return.
- One person gets a little angry, so the other one snaps back.

The problem is that while *tit for tat* is fair and just, the end result is that the relationship is over, at least for the moment.

It has broken down. There are two hurts instead of one. The sad reality is that this is the philosophy of the masses.

Getting Beyond Just Fair

So what do we do? When someone fails us, do we just act as if nothing happened? Do we take it and become doormats? Certainly not. So what is the answer?

Here is Principle Seven expressed more eloquently than I could ever attempt:

> *If you love those who love you, what credit is that to you? Even "sinners" love those who love them. And if you do good to those who are good to you, what credit is that to you? Even "sinners" do that. And if you lend to those from whom you expect repayment, what credit is that to you? Even "sinners" lend to "sinners" expecting to be repaid in full. But love your enemies, do good to them, and lend to them without expecting to get anything back.*

—LUKE 6:32–35

The answer is very simple and very hard to do: *give back better than you are given.*

THE ANSWER IS VERY SIMPLE AND VERY HARD TO DO: *GIVE BACK BETTER THAN YOU ARE GIVEN.*

People who succeed in life do not go around settling scores. They do not even keep score. They "run up the score" by doing good to others, even when the others do not deserve it. They give them better than they are given. And as a result, they often bring the other person up to their level instead of being brought down to the level of the other.

Get Rid of Anger

There are different ways of responding to anger. We'll look at two that are problematic and one that is better.

The first way to respond to your anger is to deny it, to not feel it, to not allow it to tell you that something is wrong. The other problem way of handling anger is to use it to get back at those who wrong you—to put them down, lash out, or manipulate them into improving. But such responses do not

help because they put other people on the defensive. Their anger does nothing to reach the other's heart.

Successful people know this. They do not blast people with anger. They take a third route, which is using their anger to let the other person know that there is a problem. Then they solve the problem by approaching the person in love, not anger, and facing the issue at hand. They fix problems in a way that treats the other person better than the other person treats them. In doing so, they become allies with the person to solve the problem. Successful people make their anger objective, and its object is the problem, not the person.

THE BIGGEST OBJECTION THAT PEOPLE HAVE TO GIVING GOOD WHEN THEY HAVE RECEIVED BAD IS THEIR FEAR OF BECOMING A DOORMAT.

In spite of what I've said up to this point, the biggest objection that people have to giving good when they have received bad is their fear of becoming a doormat. They think such a response is bound to result in allowing people to "get away with murder." Nothing could be further than the truth. The power of the principle is that it will improve the relationship for both parties, not just for the offending one.

Get Past Your Own Need

To make such a response requires that you get out of a basic dependent position. Goodness and maturity are not dependent on another person; they simply *are*. To possess these attributes, you must practice them regardless of how you are being treated.

GOODNESS AND MATURITY ARE NOT DEPENDENT ON ANOTHER PERSON; THEY SIMPLY *ARE*.

Hank's boss was a nightmare. In meetings he would come down on people with no warning. It was humiliating.

One day Hank was the target, but it didn't seem to faze him. He just smiled and said, "I can see what you're saying. That is helpful. I'll take that suggestion back to the design team and we'll fix it. Thanks."

A workmate was impressed. "How do you do it?" Taylor asked. "I would have lost it if he did that to me after all that hard work you put into it."

Hank answered like the successful person he was: "Well, he is just not someone I look to for approval. He doesn't have it to give. All he has is criticism, so I don't depend on him for validation. I depend on others in my own support system who know me and believe in me."

Give Others Better Than They Deserve

Not giving others what they deserve is a big part of not playing fair. To give them better than they deserve is what the Bible calls *grace*. The word means "unmerited favor". It describes how God treats us. Sometimes, as we said above, grace means that we give someone loving limits and consequences if other things have not worked. But often, limits are not needed; only a little softness is.

TO GIVE THEM BETTER THAN THEY DESERVE IS WHAT THE BIBLE CALLS *GRACE*.

Jen could have picked up Sally's dress even after Sally had not performed her side of things. She could have accepted her while still confronting the problem. However, a further thing she could have done, though, would be to extend understanding. Something like this:

"Hey, Sally. Today when you couldn't get to the check, it made me wonder if you are feeling overwhelmed with the move and everything. Do you want to talk about it? Is there some way I can make it easier for you?"

That is giving past what is deserved. That is grace. Certainly over time, if you are continually not being responded to, that could turn into being a doormat. That is not what we are talking about, however. We are just talking about doing good past where it is deserved to turn a situation around.

Few things loosen a gridlock in a relationship like asking the other person how you have hurt him or contributed to the problem. He is not expecting it.

Give the Opposite

Often we sabotage the possibility of getting what we want by giving exactly the opposite. It happens when we give just what we are given—when we are "playing fair." For example, let's assume there is someone you want to be close to, but that person disconnects and detaches. As a result, you withdraw your love. You pout or get mad. When the person attempts reconciliation later, you withhold affection when they come to you later. To give better would mean that you do not withdraw connection, but seek connection. See if you are doing

IF SOMEONE TRIES TO CONTROL YOU, DO NOT CONTROL BACK. LIVE OUT FREEDOM AND OFFER IT TO THE OTHER PERSON.

something that is driving the person away. It solves nothing to return a lack of connection with a lack of connection. If someone tries to control you, do not control back. Live out freedom and offer it to the other person. Give choices. Speak to their control issues directly by making the choices that you want to make, and do not try to manipulate them or keep them happy.

Then if she is not able to control you and gets angry, give her the same freedom that you have chosen: "I understand that my choice is frustrating to you. You can choose to be upset with me if you want. But this is what I need to do."

What Goes Around Comes Around

Successful people have transcended the need for revenge. Their first goal is to make things better for the other person or group. That does not mean they have no interest at all in their own benefit. It simply means that in their treatment of others, their goal is to do well by them *regardless of how they are treated.*

SUCCESSFUL PEOPLE HAVE TRANSCENDED THE NEED FOR REVENGE.

Solomon expressed that kind of character in this way:

Do not gloat when your enemy falls;
when he stumbles, do not let your heart rejoice,
or the LORD will see and disapprove
and turn his wrath away from him.

—PROVERBS 24:17–18

People are deeply affected when instead of justice they are showered with mercy and grace. That is like the love of God. As the Bible says, God died for us "while we were still sinners" (Romans 5:8). He loved us when we did not love him. And as a result, God wins many people over to his side through such undeserved love. They become better people and pass that love on to others.

What happens when it does not work out? Successful people are not tied to doing just what is "fair." They are free to move on. They do not need to settle the score. They let it go and get on about their business. Because of that, they are not forever held up in the past, bitter, or dragged down by old hurts and grievances that are still alive in their souls. Forgiving and letting go have set them free.

Be Humble

If you can't laugh at yourself,
then who can you laugh at?

— TIGER WOODS

Ryan was a young executive with a Fortune 500 company. I had heard the story of how in a short amount of time he took an almost nonexistent laundry soap business in China to one with sales of nearly a billion dollars. I asked him how he did it. I did not expect the answer he gave. "I got a job on a rice farm," he said. "What?" I asked, a little confused.

Although Ryan was known as something of a soap expert, he didn't know how the typical Chinese worker used the product. "So I figured that in order to sell it to them, I had better understand them first."

It turns out that the water in most Chinese homes was very hard, but there were a few special places where they could go to find softer water. "The softer water would cause the detergent to create more suds, which would result in better cleaning and use less soap as well," he said. So most workers took an inconvenient trip to wash their clothes in soft water.

He took that information back to the research department, which developed a detergent formula that made as many suds with hard water as it did with soft. So for the first time, they could do their wash at home. It was a revolution of sorts.

"Then we created some ads that showed all those bubbles using the water within their homes, and we were off. Sales skyrocketed to $800 million," he said.

So that explains it: the way to sell soap in China is to work on a rice farm. Or does it?

The real answer is the one to a more important question: what attitude made my friend conceive of the idea to work on a rice farm and then be willing to do it? The answer: *humility*.

It was humility that made a billion dollars, not soap or rice. This simple but profound quality of humility is the eighth of the Nine Things, and it helps people succeed in both love and accomplishment.

The Need to Be Greater Than We Are

We've seen that we must dig up and invest our talents, and move past the negative. We know we must make decisions based on their effects, and always ask how to improve a situation whether or not it's our responsibility. We achieve our goals through small steps, and protect the good with a healthy hatred. Principle Eight, *be humble*, has enormous implications.

Often we miss the ways that humility contributes to success in work and relationships. Part of the reason for this is that

MOST PEOPLE CAN "SMELL" TRUE HUMILITY AS WELL AS THE STENCH OF ARROGANCE OR PRIDE THAT IS ITS OPPOSITE.

our thinking is sometimes a little fuzzy about what it means to be humble. Most people can "smell" true humility as well as the stench of arrogance or pride that is its opposite. We know it when we see it.

But how do we understand humility in ways that we can put into practice? One simple, guiding principle that encompasses many others is this: *humility is not having a need to be more than you are.*

When I think of how the successful person performs in the arena of humility, that is a pretty good description—to just be who he or she really is, a human being like everyone else, avoiding the need to be more than that.

Think of people you have worked with who came into the

company with a know-it-all attitude. Are they still there? Often not. Were they liked? Probably not. What was it like to talk to them? Did you feel listened to? Understood? Valued? Did you want to go to the mat and sacrifice for them? Hardly.

The arrogant ones who think they know before they know are always tough to deal with. And though they might

---

HUMILITY IS NOT HAVING A NEED TO BE MORE THAN YOU ARE.

---

appear successful for a short time, arrogant people ultimately fail to be successful in work because they never learn what they do not know. And they fail at relationships because they never learn that people do not like them before it is too late.

Just as humility sells soap, it can also build success in all areas of your life. Let's look at some of the important ways that humility contributes to success, and how lacking it can guarantee failure.

Humility Identifies with Others

Once, when I had failed miserably in a business situation, an older hero of mine happened to call me. He had been an important figure in my business life and had coached me over the years. He was very successful, and it was a little embarrassing for him to phone right then. I wanted to hide.

But when I explained the way that I had screwed things up, he just listened. I kind of expected him to say, "What an idiot. I can't believe I wasted time on you!" or at least think it. What he said, however, totally turned things around. He said, "Well, we've all been there."

SUCCESSFUL PEOPLE UNDERSTAND FAILURE, AND THEY DID NOT GET TO BE SUCCESSFUL WITHOUT A FEW FAILURES OF THEIR OWN.

I couldn't believe it. What that did for me was show me that successful people understand failure, and they did not get to be successful without a few failures of their own. It helped me to see that what I was going through was a normal part of the path of success. I saw that one of the reasons he was so successful was that he was not surprised or thrown off by failure.

**ACCEPT YOUR OWN FAILURES AND MISTAKES,
AND SEE THEM AS PART OF THE PROCESS.**

My friend had learned a critical key to success: *accept your own failures and mistakes, and see them as part of the process.* Successful people see failures as inevitable and as natural. Identifying with other normal humans who fail leads to a number of success patterns, as we shall continue to see. The first two of these are huge factors in achieving success:

1. Successful people show kindness, understanding, and help to others who fail.

2. Successful people are not derailed by their failures; they accept them as a normal part of the process.

The first certainly is an incredible gift to others. Over and over I have seen how successful people extend themselves to serve others. Truly successful people are givers, period. Success and giving are synonyms in many ways. Always.

But beyond being an obvious gift to others, humble givers also develop a lot of relational equity over time. They have extended themselves to understand and reach out to others, and as a result they are highly appreciated and loved. They give freely and not to get anything in return; yet they are truly appreciated and *do* get a lot in return.

The big result is that humble givers are deeply loved and never alone in the world. And there is no higher success than that—to have deep, quality friends over time, friends that you are there for and who are there for you. This *is* success, and it also leads to other successes, as you will always need the support of other people to accomplish whatever you do in life.

PEOPLE WHO WIN IN LIFE DO NOT CONDEMN THEMSELVES FOR FAILURE; THEY ACCEPT IT.

The second point mentioned earlier is huge for success as well. *People who win in life do not condemn themselves for failure; they accept it.* They learn from it. Failure motivates them to do better. They do not beat themselves up for it, and they do not begin to believe that they cannot accomplish something just because they failed. Because they are humble and identify with the human race that makes mistakes and fails, they see failure as normal. They use it and do not feel disqualified because of it. It is a paradox of monumental proportions.

> **YOUR FAILURE OF THE MOMENT**
> **DOES NOT MEAN ANYTHING**
> **IN TERMS OF YOUR ABILITY**
> **TO FINALLY "MAKE IT."**

Self-confidence does not come from seeing yourself as strong, without flaws. Self-confidence and belief in yourself comes from accepting your mistakes and realizing that you can grow past them and learn from them. You realize that your failure of the moment does not mean anything in terms of your ability to finally "make it."

The Biggest Sickness of All

People who think they have it all together are infected with a terrible sickness, and they do not even know it. As David said, they flatter themselves too much to see where they miss the mark (Psalm 36:2). They are not wise in other areas, either, because their wish to be seen as perfect keeps them from seeing other realities outside themselves as well.

WISE PEOPLE . . . KNOW THEIR WEAKNESSES.

Wise people, in contrast, know their weaknesses. They do not have the sickness of trying to preserve a view that they are all good, either in their own minds or in the eyes of others, because they do not have such a view. Nor do they desire that others have that view of them.

Regarding their imperfections, these people do at least two things very well that build success, foster good relationships, and encourage learning, growth, and wisdom:

1. They admit it quickly when they are wrong.
2. They receive correction and confrontation from others well.

The first quality aids in learning and is always correlated

with wisdom. We cannot grow and learn if we cannot admit our mistakes.

In a conference I was leading, an executive named Adam had just outlined his current situation to the group. One of the group members asked him, "Would you like some feedback?" We could all tell from his expression that what he had to say would not be complementary.

Adam's response was outstanding, "Of course; *give me a gift*." Though he anticipated criticism was coming, he welcomed it. He realized that getting correction by someone wise was a gift indeed. That is a consistent mark of wise people. They are not defensive to feedback. Defensiveness is the mark of a fool. Here is how Solomon saw it:

> *A mocker resents correction;*
> *he will not consult the wise.*
> —PROVERBS 15:12

A prideful spirit that resists correction makes for bad relationships. And past that, it makes for a lack of success in the life of the defensive person.

Giving It Up and Gaining It All

Humility could be seen as giving up the need to be greater than we are. It is giving up thinking that we know it all. Giving up thinking that we can do it all. Giving up thinking that we have to do it well all the time. Giving up the need to be seen as right or good all the time, and giving up defensiveness. Humility is seeing a true picture of ourselves.

HUMILITY IS SEEING A TRUE PICTURE OF OURSELVES.

This does not imply the need for self-deprecation, such as, "Oh, it was really nothing," after a huge accomplishment. A simple "thank you" is a wonderful response.

Learn the way of humility. When you do, not only will you succeed more, but you will also keep your success as well. Here are a few tips:

- Say you are sorry when you fail others.
- Get rid of any defensiveness.
- The moment you think some task or position is beneath

you, take a time-out. Go and spend time with someone performing that task, and you might meet a human being superior to yourself.

- Root out any attitude of entitlement that you have. Embrace a spirit of gratitude.
- When someone is hurt by you, listen. Try to understand their feelings.
- Embrace and anticipate your imperfections and the imperfections of others.

Be humble.

Upset the Right People

Avoid popularity if you would have peace.

— ABRAHAM LINCOLN

Simon had been hired to turn the company around. But there was one problem. To do it, he was going to have to make some very hard decisions that people were not going to be happy with. Some would be laid off, and others would have to move. It was going to be a stormy time. The other part of it was that many of them were Simon's friends. But it was a dire situation, and there was little question that for the company to make it, it was the right decision.

I wondered if he could do it. He loved people, and I knew that he would hate to hurt anyone. He was in a tough place. But he surprised me. Simon made the tough decisions, and he turned the company around. In fact, it could be argued that he saved it. Along the way, however, people were indeed very upset with him for his decisions. I asked him about it.

"Well, there were always two parts to this. One was what the right thing to do was. The other was how people were going to feel about that. As long as I made sure that those were two separate issues, I could deal with each of them correctly. If I got them confused, then I might make the wrong decision based on how people would feel if I made the right one," he explained.

> ### *SUCCESSFUL PEOPLE DO NOT MAKE DECISIONS BASED ON THE FEAR OF OTHER PEOPLE'S REACTIONS.*

And that was the key to Simon's success. He did not make his decision based on how people would feel. He made it based on what was right.

Successful people do not make decisions based on the fear of other people's reactions.

> ### THEY DECIDE TO DO WHAT IS RIGHT FIRST AND DEAL WITH THE FALLOUT SECOND.

Successful people who practice Principle Nine are sensitive to those reactions, but when weighing whether or not a given course is right, whether or not someone else is going to like it, is not a factor that carries any weight. They care about other people's feelings, but they do not base their decisions on them. They decide to do what is right first and deal with the fallout second.

Think of situations where being overly concerned about hurting someone's feelings can cause a person to stall out or drag a bad thing on too long:

- Confronting a person
- Saying no to a request to do something that involves time, energy, money, or other resources
- Doing an intervention with someone because of her destructive behavior
- Telling a person that he has overstayed his welcome
- Breaking up with the person you are dating

The Difference between Hurt and Harm

One of the important distinctions that wise people make is to understand the difference between hurting someone and harming him. Hurt is a normal part of life. Our feelings can be hurt when we get confronted, for example. But it hurts like surgery hurts: it is good for us. The confrontation hurts, but it does not injure or harm us. Harm is when we injure people by doing destructive things to them.

After All I've Done for You . . .

Another barrier that many people feel when making decisions is guilt. When they choose to do something for themselves, or make any kind of decision based on their conviction that it is the right thing to do, they sometimes feel as if they have done something bad because of people's adverse reactions.

Kelly had a tough decision after graduating. She was offered a job in another city, and that would take her away from her Aunt Carrie, who had helped her a lot in school. But the job was a great opportunity. She knew her aunt would not want to see her go, but Carrie would be fine without her. Although Kelly would miss her aunt, it was the right move to make. Unfortunately, that's not how Aunt Carrie saw it.

"Well, isn't that gratitude," Aunt Carrie said. "After all I have done to help you through school, the first chance you get to move away, you take it. Great. Really shows appreciation, leaving the ones who help you."

Kelly was stunned. Nevertheless, although it would be tough to work out, she knew what was best and she was going to have to make the move.

Do Not Rescue an Angry Man

That is the thing to remember about trying to appease controlling and angry people. If you let their anger decide your course of action, then you have just trained them in how to get what they want out of you. You have set yourself up for the same experience again.

THERE IS A DIRECT CORRELATION WITH PEOPLE WHO ARE OUT OF CONTROL IN THEIR LIVES AND THEIR HATRED OF THE WORD *NO*.

There is a direct correlation with people who are out of control in their lives and their hatred of the word *no*. You do not usually see responsible people get angry and attack simply because they do not get their way. But often you do see irresponsible people get mad when they hear the word *no*.

Loss of Approval or Love

Sometimes those who need to confront are afraid of not only a negative response such as anger or guilt, but the loss of something positive that they value too highly to risk.

Josh's dad owned a very successful business. The father assumed that his only son would follow in his footsteps and succeed him as president of the company. But in college, John received a different call. He was determined to become a minister. His dad was furious, saying that if Josh were a "real man," as he put it, Josh would do a "real man's job."

Through his character and the strength God gave him, Josh did not change his course. He was saddened by the loss of his father's approval, but he saw that approval as a separate issue from the decision itself. If he were weak, like his father said he was, then he would have caved and followed his father's wishes. The reality was exactly the opposite. His strength was what enabled him to do what this father perceived as less manly.

Years have passed, and Josh and his dad have reconciled. The son's ministry has grown, and his father is very proud of him. The story would have had a very different ending if Josh had given in instead of sticking to his course.

Successful people go against the odds if the odds are

against what is right. They are willing to be the odd one, risking loss of approval in order to do the right thing. They

---

SUCCESSFUL PEOPLE GO AGAINST THE ODDS IF THE ODDS ARE AGAINST WHAT IS RIGHT.

---

understand that the approval of others does not go very far in making one truly fulfilled. It may be nice for a moment, but getting up every day and doing what you believe in is much more lasting.

Learning to Upset the Right People

The key is not to count your critics, but instead to weigh them. If kind, loving, responsible, and honest people are upset with you, then you had better look at the choices you are making. But if controlling, hot and cold, irresponsible, or manipulative people are upset with you, then take courage! That might be a sign that you are doing the right thing!

Jesus said it best: "Woe to you when all men speak well of you" (Luke 6:26). When all people speak well of you, it means that you are duplicitous and a people-pleaser. You cannot speak the truth, live out good values, and choose your own direction without disappointing some people.

DO NOT TRY TO AVOID UPSETTING PEOPLE.

JUST MAKE SURE THAT YOU ARE

UPSETTING THE RIGHT ONES.

Do not try to avoid upsetting people. *Just make sure that you are upsetting the right ones.*

The Sky Is the Limit

*All we have to decide is what to do
with the time that is given to us.*

—J. R. R. TOLKIEN,
THE FELLOWSHIP OF THE RING

I will never forget that day. I was sitting in my college dorm room and everything looked pretty dark to me. I had gone to school with high hopes for a sports career, but that dream was chronically hampered and finally ended by a tendon injury. After the injury I had tried to find an alternative, something I wanted to do and could really sink my teeth into. But I was having no luck. It seemed that none of the courses I took and none of the areas I looked into really grabbed me.

To make my mood even darker, I had just gone through a breakup with a girlfriend with whom I was quite serious. It made me wonder how a good relationship is found or made to last. At that moment, success seemed pretty unattainable to me, both in love and life.

Then for some reason, I had the thought that I should look in the Bible. That was not something I had done much since arriving at college. I was too deeply involved in other things to think about my spiritual life. But on that day I was at the bottom, so when the thought came I was more open to spiritual direction than usual.

When I opened the book, I came upon a verse that seemed to jump out at me. It was from a section where Jesus was saying that worrying about life (exactly what I was doing at that moment) does not get us very far in accomplishing the life that we desire. Instead, he pointed to a different path:

> *So do not worry, saying, "What shall we eat?"*
> *or "What shall we drink?" or "What shall we*
> *wear?" For the pagans run after all these*
> *things, and your heavenly Father knows that*
> *you need them. But seek first his kingdom and*
> *his righteousness, and all these things will be*
> *given to you as well. Therefore do not worry*
> *about tomorrow, for tomorrow will worry*
> *about itself. Each day has enough trouble of*
> *its own.*
> —MATTHEW 6:31–34

On that particular day, I did not know all of what Jesus meant in those verses, but I did know that the way I was going about things was not working. So I decided to try it his way. I told him that I wanted help. I guess you could call it that "leap of faith" that people talk about. In my naiveté, I was hoping he might just come down and make it all better. And in a real sense, that is exactly what he did. But *how* he did it was far from what I expected. There were no lightning bolts, no instructions written across the sky.

GOD PUTS PEOPLE IN OUR LIVES
WHO SHOW US THE WAY.

What he did was this: immediately God put people around me who knew the path I was seeking and who helped me to go step by step onto that path. I discovered a great truth, and all the successful people I have ever known have told me it has been true for them as well: *God puts people in our lives who show us the way.*

These God-sent people are models for us. They show us how to grow and what steps to take. They push us, correct us, support us, and discipline us. And as they do all of that, we have to do some things as well: we have to become what God and others are showing us we need to be. We have to be engaged in the process and take the steps to become whom he created us to be. That is the meaning of the part of the verse about seeking his kingdom and his righteousness. It means we need to learn his ways and become a person who learns more and more how to do it "right."

On that day I discovered four things that changed my life. They were the same four things I have heard other people affirm countless times:

1. God is there to help us if we ask him.
2. He not only helps us directly, but he gives us others to help as well.
3. There are truths and principles that are the ways he designed life to work.
4. As we practice those ways, good things are given.

Jesus said that the one who asks, seeks, and knocks will receive. Prayer is simple conversation with God, the source of all that we need. He knows the answers to our dilemmas, he knows where the resources we need are to be found, and he knows the ways in which we need to change. If you ask him, he will answer.

This is no magic formula or quick fix. Often we do not even see his answers except in retrospect. But he always answers, and his answers are always for our good, even when they do not seem that way at the moment.

While you are performing any task, be asking him all the while for help. You will be surprised at how present God becomes in every area of your life.

If you have never met Jesus and desire a relationship with him, he told us how to do it and issued each person a challenge to find out whether he is real or not. He said, "Here I am! I stand at the door and knock. If anyone hears my voice and opens the door, I will come in and eat with him, and he with me" (Revelation 3:20).

Jesus claimed to be God, and he claims to be alive today. Test this claim for yourself. Ask him sincerely if he really is alive and really is there. If you do this, he will show up. You will never be alone again if you put your trust in him as Messiah and Lord. Then, ask him to relieve you of your worries and help you along the path toward what you are trying to accomplish. He promises to be a Shepherd to you for the rest of your life.

The Nine Things Are for *You*

I want to leave you with a reminder of one thing I said in the beginning. It is something that watching my wise friends taught me: *the Nine Things we have discussed in these chapters are available to us all.*

SUCCESS IS AVAILABLE TO ALL
WHO JOIN GOD AND HIS WAYS.

Therefore, success is not for only a few, or some accident that just happens to some. Success is available to all who join God and his ways. Just like gravity can make someone soar above the clouds, learning and working the "ways" of success can enable you to reach past anything you thought possible for your future. The sky literally is the limit.

I hope that this book has been helpful to you. I would encourage you to look to God, ask for his help, and put the ways into practice that you have learned here. Never give up, and never stop seeking to be all God created you to be.

God Bless.

—Henry